FUN
with
MODELING
CLAY

By Barbara Reid

KIDS CAN PRESS

To Ian, Zoe and Tara — BR

Published in Canada by
Kids Can Press Ltd.
29 Birch Avenue
Toronto, ON M4V 1E2

Published in the U.S. by
Kids Can Press Ltd.
85 River Rock Drive, Suite 202
Buffalo, NY 14207

Edited by Valerie Wyatt
Designed by Karen Powers
Printed in Hong Kong by Wing King Tong Co. Ltd.

CM 98 0 9 8 7 6 5 4 3 2 1

Canadian Cataloguing in Publication Data
Reid, Barbara, 1957–
Fun with modeling clay
(Kids Can crafts)
ISBN 1-55074-510-7
1. Modeling - Juvenile literature. 2. Clay - Juvenile literature. I. Title. II. Series.
TT916.R44 1998   j731.4'2   C97-931624-3

3MB L0000054932

Contents

About modeling clay

What would you like to make? A two-headed dinosaur? A scary, green-faced witch? A lump of modeling clay and a good imagination is all you need to make characters and pictures that are funny, silly, wild and crazy, or beautiful.

There are many different types of clay. Some are water-based and will dry out if you leave them uncovered. Others are meant to be baked into a permanent shape. The suggestions in this book will work best with modeling clay, an oily, squishable clay that never gets hard, even after sitting untouched for a year. Plasticine, Plastolina, Klean Klay and Plasticolor are a few of the brands you may find at your local arts and crafts or toy store.

TIPS

- No matter how careful you are, some clay may fall on the carpet. Pick it up right away: it's almost impossible to get off once someone has stepped on it.

- Crumbs and dirt will stick to modeling clay and make it unpleasant to work with. To keep it clean, store the clay in plastic containers when you're not using it.

- One of the best things about modeling clay is that you can change it. If what you're making isn't turning out the way you want, squash it up and try again.

- Modeling clay comes in many different colors. You can mix colors by squishing and kneading two pieces together until they blend into one new, smooth color. Experiment and invent your own shades.

- Once some colors have become really stuck together, you'll never be able to separate them. Sometimes this gives a nice marbled effect. If you'd rather have one solid color, blend the pieces together over and over until you get a ball of one color, probably a dull gray-brown.

TOOLS YOU'LL NEED

A BOARD

You will need a smooth, hard surface to work on. Modeling clay is oily, so don't use it on a surface it could damage. Kitchen tables are often ideal. Or try to get a big piece of Masonite board or illustration board (a type of stiff cardboard sold at art supply stores).

A KNIFE

Modeling clay is very soft so you don't need a sharp knife. Even a nail file or the edge of a ruler will work to cut the shapes you need.

ROUND PENCILS

The point of a pencil can be used to make many kinds of textures and dots. A round pencil can also be used as a roller, to flatten clay.

WIRES, PAPER CLIPS, TOOTHPICKS

These are handy for cutting, poking and prodding the clay into the shapes you want. Pieces of toothpick can also be inserted into tall, thin shapes to strengthen them.

YOUR HANDS

These are probably the most useful tools. They help warm up the clay and make it easier to shape. Fingernails can cut clay and make little curved lines and textures on the surface.

TOOLS FOR SPECIAL EFFECTS

Combs, garlic presses, toothbrushes and pieces of textured cloth can give some really neat effects. Make sure it's okay with the owner before you use them. (Sometimes modeling clay is hard to get off things.)

Use your imagination and you'll find all sorts of objects that can become part of your tool bag.

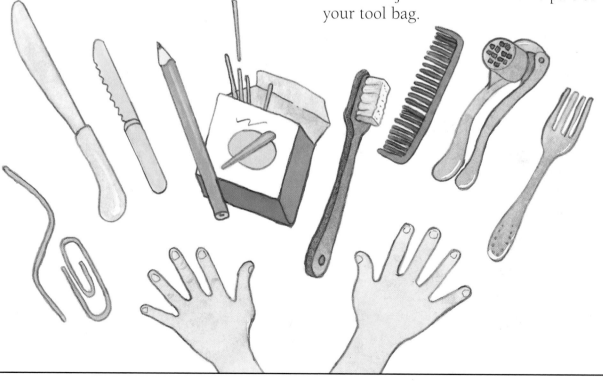

Basic shapes

All modeling-clay creations begin as small lumps of clay. By practicing the basic shapes shown here, you'll get an idea of what modeling clay can do. And you can combine these shapes to make almost anything you can imagine. Of course there are lots of other shapes you can make, but these will get you started.

To begin, roll and knead a small piece of clay for a few minutes to warm it up and make it soft and smooth.

BALL

Form a rough ball with your fingers and roll it round and round between your palms. The more you roll it, the smoother it will become. Try making balls of different sizes.

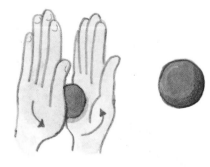

EGG

Start with a round ball. Gently roll it up and down with your palms. When it has become a longer oval shape, round the ends with your fingers to form a smooth egg.

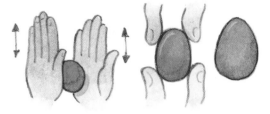

PANCAKE

You can make a pancake from a ball. Just flatten it between your thumb and finger. If the edge cracks, smooth over the cracks with your fingers. Try making different sizes and thicknesses.

DROP

Pinch one side of a ball into a point. Turn the shape around in your fingers and keep pinching the point until the clay looks like a nice fat drop of water.

CONE

Press the big end of a drop onto your board to give it a flat bottom. Smooth the sides to form an even cone shape.

SNAKE

To make this very useful shape, roll a piece of clay back and forth on the board until it gets long and thin. The more you roll it, the longer and thinner it will become.

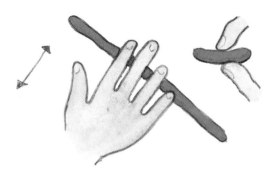

SAUSAGE

A sausage is just a short, thick snake.

CYLINDER

To make a cylinder, cut the ends of a sausage with a knife. Or roll out a short, fat sausage and press each end flat on the board.

BOX

Place a short cylinder on its side and gently press it with another small, smooth board or anything flat. Roll it over so that the flat part is on the side and press it again. It should now have four flat sides. Stand the box on end and press again. Turn and press the sides of the box again to change the box's height.

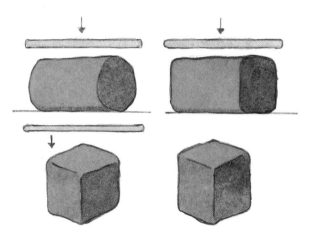

RIBBON

Make a snake about the size of a pencil. Lay it on the board and roll a round pencil back and forth over it. Don't make the ribbon too thin. Carefully peel the ribbon from the board.

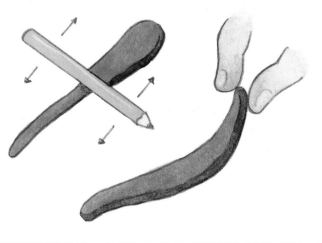

ANIMALS

Start off with simple animal shapes and before you know it you'll have a whole zooful of creatures. Remember to press firmly when you have to stick two parts together, such as a leg to a body, so that they won't fall apart later.

Snakes and bugs

Take some simple shapes and turn them into snakes and other creepy crawlies.

SNAKE

1 Roll out a snake shape. Roll one end into a point to form the tail.

2 Roll out a smaller, thin snake for a tongue. Fold this piece in half. Leave the ends spread apart and pinch and roll the folded part smooth.

3 Attach the tongue to the bottom of the snake's head. Make two small balls for eyes and press them onto the head. Draw on a mouth with the point of a pencil.

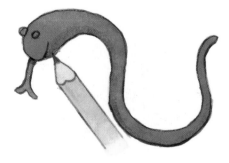

4 Decorate your snake with small pancake spots and curl him into any position.

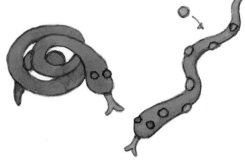

SPIDER

1 To make a spider, lightly press a ball of clay onto the board to flatten the bottom. Stick on a smaller ball for a head and add a face.

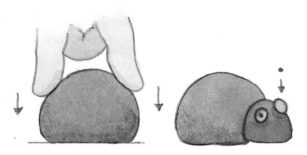

2 Roll out eight thin snakes for legs. Pick up the spider and attach the legs onto its flat bottom.

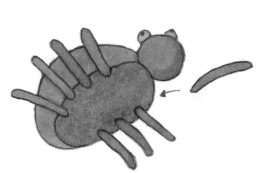

LADYBUG

1 Press together two eggs of the same size. Pinch them together at the top and bottom.

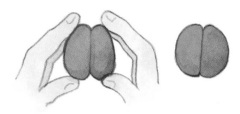

2 Lightly press the shell onto the board to flatten the bottom. Add a head and eyes. Press on six thin snakes for legs, two for feelers and some small pancake spots.

OTHER IDEAS

● Create some weird and wonderful bugs of your own. Dot them, stripe them and experiment with their shapes. How about adding wings?

Leaping lizards

Whether they're shelled, scaly, spiny or slippery, reptiles are great to make out of modeling clay.

TURTLE

1 To make a turtle, start with a thick pancake for the bottom shell. Add four sausage legs, a bigger sausage head and a small sausage tail.

2 Make another, slightly bigger pancake for the top shell. Press it over the bottom shell so that it's slightly rounded.

3 Use a sharp pencil to dot in some eyes and add texture to the shell.

CROCODILE

1 Roll a thick snake with a pointed tail. With a knife or wire, carefully cut the head end open to about one third of the way along the body.

2 Stick two small balls on the end of the snout and dot in nostrils with a pencil. Add two bigger balls on the head for eyes. Starting at the back of the mouth, add some curved cones for teeth.

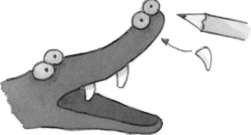

3 Four sausages become legs. Add some claws. Bend the croc's body and tail into whatever position you want.

4 To make scales, start at the tail end and press on a row of small pancakes. Add a second row so that it barely overlaps the first. Keep overlapping rows until the area you want to be scaly is covered.

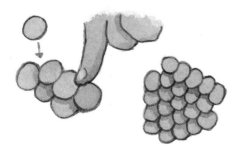

5 Draw some squiggly lines down the reptile's back with a sharp pencil for a different kind of texture.

OTHER IDEAS

● Combine scales and spikes with different head and tail shapes and invent a whole world of reptiles.

Birds of a feather

Start with a basic bird and create a whole flock of fabulous flyers by adding different kinds of feathers, wings, tails and beaks.

BASIC BIRD

1 To make a bird's body, press a drop shape onto the board to give it a flat bottom. Tip it slightly so that the pointed end (the tail) is up. Add a ball for the head.

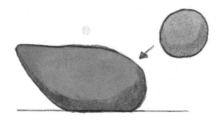

2 For wings, make two smaller drops and flatten them. Press a wing onto each side of the bird's body.

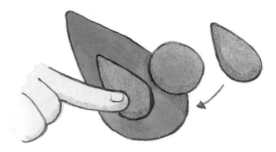

3 Stick a cone shape onto the head for a beak. The beak can be short or long, fat or thin, curved or straight. Dot in some eyes.

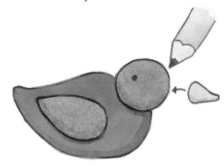

4 Press flattened sausage shapes onto the tail for fancy tail feathers. Add two small balls for feet.

DUCK

1 To turn the basic bird shape into a duck, press two flat ovals together and attach them to the bird's head (instead of the cone) for a bill.

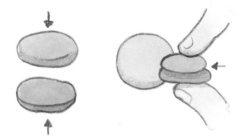

2 A duck's flat webbed feet can be made from two flattened triangles. Don't forget to make the duck's tail curve up.

GOOSE

Change a duck to a goose by adding a neck. Attach a short snake for the neck, but be sure it's thick enough to support the head.

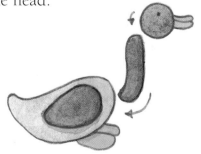

SWAN

Swans have long, curving necks and smaller bills. Their wings are bigger and point up, over the back.

OTHER IDEAS

● Make some fanciful birds by adding wild tail feathers or colorful crests on their heads.

● If you leave the feet off your ducks, geese and swans and put them on a mirror, you can create a duck pond.

Sitting pretty

Begin by making a sitting cat, then try other animal "sitters."

CAT

1 Roll out an egg shape and press the bigger end onto the board so that it stands up.

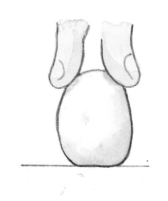

2 Attach a pancake to the bottom half of each side of the egg to make the back legs.

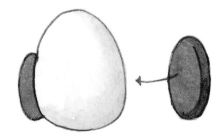

3 Add a small sausage foot to the bottom of each pancake. Add two longer sausages to the front of the body about three-quarters of the way up. These are the front legs.

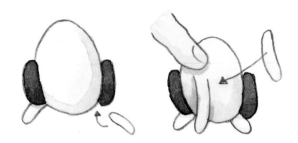

4 Add a round ball to the top of the egg for a head. To make ears, make two small drop shapes and press one onto each side of the head.

5 Press two small pancakes together onto the bottom half of the cat's face for a muzzle. Add a small ball to the bottom of the muzzle for a chin and another to the top of the muzzle for a nose.

6 Attach two ovals to the cat's face for eyes. Draw a short line down each oval with a sharp pencil to make the pupil. Draw on some whiskers.

7 Add a sausage tail to complete your cat. You can turn the cat's head or add a tongue. Add some thin snake shapes to make your cat striped.

LION

What would happen to the cat if it grew a mane and a tassel on the end of its tail?

MOUSE

Change a cat into a mouse. For the head make a drop shape and add a little mouse nose at the end. Two pancakes become ears. Add small front paws and draw on eyes and whiskers.

OTHER ANIMALS

Play around with different sorts of heads and tails to make a rabbit, squirrel, beaver or kangaroo.

Four-legged friends

Start by making a sausage dog out of a sausage shape, then put some other animals on their feet.

DOG

1 Roll one large sausage for the body and one long snake to cut into four equal pieces for the legs. Lay the body on the board and stick on the legs.

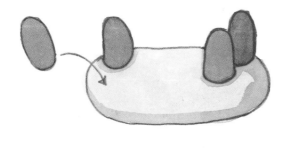

2 Turn the whole thing over and gently press down to make the legs even. Wiggle it around a little until it's steady. Add a small sausage tail.

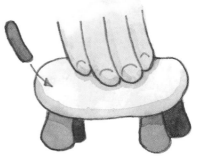

3 Add a round ball on top of the other end for a head. Press a stubby cylinder onto the front of the head for a snout.

4 Carefully cut the snout through the middle with a wire or knife. Open this mouth carefully with your fingers. Stick a small ball on for a nose and add a tiny sausage tongue.

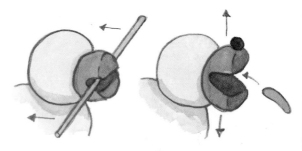

5 Add one flattened triangle to each side of the head for ears. Attach two small balls for eyes and dot in the pupils with a sharp pencil.

6 Change the body, ear, tail and snout shapes to make all sorts of dogs. Cover your dog with minipancake spots, or scratch on some lines with a sharp pencil for fur.

FOX

If you use a drop shape for a head, cones for ears, and a very fat drop shape for a tail, a dog will become one of its cousins.

RACCOON

1 Start with a short, fat body, a pointed head, pointed ears and two dark pancakes for the raccoon's mask. Add balls on top of the mask for eyes.

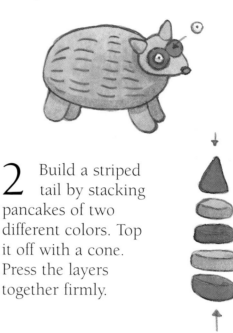

2 Build a striped tail by stacking pancakes of two different colors. Top it off with a cone. Press the layers together firmly.

3 Turn the tail on its side and roll the edges smooth. Pinch it into a bushy-tail shape and attach it to the body.

A zooful of animals

Let your imagination run wild and make all kinds of animals. Just remember that the bigger the body, the sturdier the legs must be.

BEAR

1 Start with an egg shape and add four thick cylinder legs. Add a small tail at one end and a ball head at the other.

2 Make a snout like a dog's (see step 3, page 16). Add small half-pancake ears and dot in the eyes with a sharp pencil.

PIG

1 Start with a fat egg and four sausage legs. Add a curly tail, ball eyes and a cylinder snout with nostril holes.

2 Make each ear by pinching one side of a small pancake and pressing the pinched part onto the head. Or use a pencil to poke them into place.

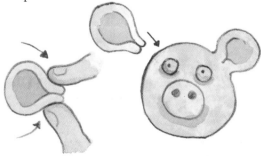

ELEPHANT

1 Start with a fat egg for a body and four thick cylinders for legs. For the head and trunk, roll a ball and pinch a small part of it between your fingers.

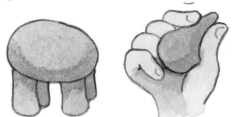

2 Roll and pull this trunk until it's the right length, and dot nostrils at the end. Attach the head. Add two big pancake ears, two small tusks and a tiny tail.

HORSE AND FRIENDS

Horses, zebras and giraffes all have long, thin legs. To help them stand up, make the feet big, or try sticking the two front legs or the two back legs together.

SEAL

1 Make a big drop shape and pinch the round end into a point. Bend one end up and forward to make an S shape. With a knife or wire, carefully split the tail end into two flippers.

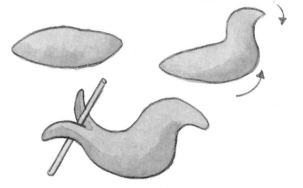

2 Spread the flippers and pinch them flat. Add a flipper-shaped triangle on each side, where the body bends. The points of the flippers should touch the board.

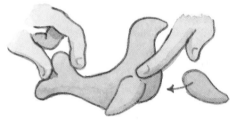

3 For a mouth, cut the point of the head with a knife and open it slightly. With a sharp pencil, dot on some eyes. Add a round ball for a nose.

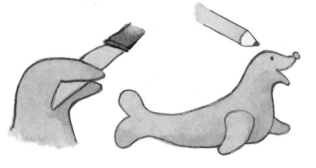

PEOPLE

It's difficult to make clay people stand up because they only have two legs. Thick legs and long feet will help. Or try gently inserting a piece of toothpick up each leg of your finished figure to stiffen it. You can also prop your figures against chairs or other objects.

Body building

Clay people can be simple or very detailed. Start with two simple "people": a snowman and a robot. Then try building the real thing.

SNOWMAN

Build a clay snowman like a real one, but with toothpick arms, a clay ribbon scarf and a clay minicarrot nose. A cylinder on top of a pancake makes a great hat.

ROBOT

To make a robot, put together a box body and head and some cylinders. Make bolts with small pencil dots or tiny balls.

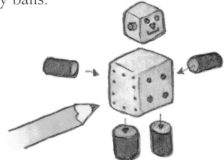

PERSON

1 For a basic human, begin with a short, fat cylinder body. Flatten it slightly so that you have a back and a front.

2 Roll a snake and fold it in half for legs. Press the folded end onto the body. Turn the ends of the legs up slightly to form feet.

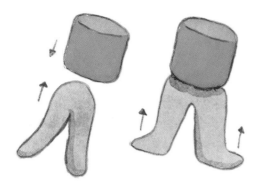

3 To stand the figure up, hold on to the legs and feet and press the figure onto the board. If your figure wobbles, try thicker legs or shorter ones or stick the legs together.

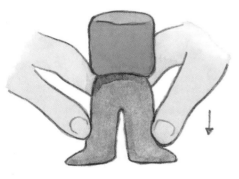

4 Arms can be made from two sausages, one attached at each shoulder. A round ball on top becomes the head.

5 To make a hand, start with a small ball and pinch out and roll a thin thumb of clay. Flatten the hand part into a pancake and bend the thumb alongside the palm.

6 This mitten-like hand can be attached to the arm. You can even cut fingers into it with a knife.

7 To add a face, poke in eyes with a sharp pencil, add a tiny ball nose and press in a fingernail smile.

Dressing up

People come in many shapes and sizes, and their clothes change the way they look. Here are some ideas to try out on the basic person you made on page 21.

SKIRTS

Use a drop shape or an egg to make a skirt. A long skirt, in place of legs, will help your person stand up.

SHORTER SKIRTS

Make a large, thin pancake and shape it over your finger. Push the legs up under it. This shape can also form a cape or hat.

BALLET TUTU

Attach a thick pancake to the body before you add on the legs. Make it frilly by pressing a wire into the edge all the way around.

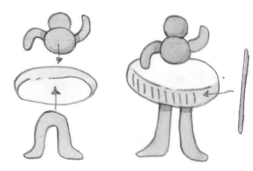

SHORTS

Bend a short snake in half and flatten the ends. Stick on legs.

FOOTWEAR

Your people can wear anything from tall boots to flat triangle flippers. Elves might wear slippers with curled-up toes that have a bell on the end.

COLLARS AND SCARVES

Add a pancake collar between the head and body or wrap your person up with a snake or ribbon scarf.

HATS

Combine cones, cylinders, pancakes and eggs to make all sorts of hats.

FINISHING TOUCHES

Don't forget buttons, bows and belts. And you can make polka dots out of small pancakes or draw on stripes or plaids with a sharp pencil.

OTHER IDEAS

● For some real fun, try making clowns — they have interesting body shapes and clothes. Or experiment with your own favorites, such as witches, Vikings, hockey players or princesses.

Face it!

Here are some ideas to help you turn a basic face into one that's special, spooky or just silly. Start with the face you made on page 21.

EARS

Make a small sausage and curve it into a **C** shape. Press it onto the head. What if you're making an alien with big pointed ears? Experiment!

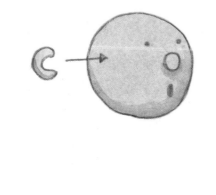

MOUTHS

Make lips out of thin snakes. These snake lips can show many expressions. For a vampire, add pointy fangs.

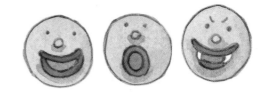

OPEN MOUTHS

Carve into the head with a knife. Cut out a slice to make the mouth wide open. The deeper the cut, the bigger the mouth. A flat sausage makes a good tongue.

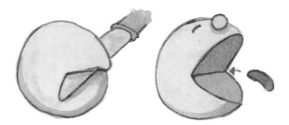

NOSES

Press a cone-shaped nose onto the head and poke in nostrils with a sharp pencil. Play around with other noses — long ones, curved ones, fat ones and turned-up ones.

EYES

For large eyes, try a small ball with a pencil dot or another small ball as a pupil. These eyes can look in any direction. Add eyelashes or eyebrows.

NECKS AND HEADS

Eggs, balls, drops and other shapes can be used for heads. Use a cylinder to make a neck.

CHEEKS

Small pancakes make good cheeks. And don't forget about tiny pancake freckles.

HAIRSTYLES

- Wrap a big, thin pancake over a head. Add some sausage pigtails.

- Cover a head with long, thin snakes. Braid them if you wish.

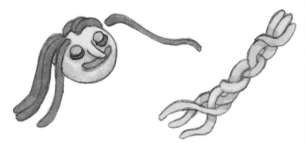

- Curly hair can be made with coiled snakes or with cylinders or round balls.

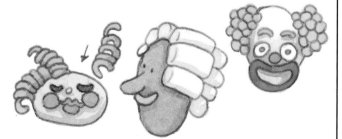

- Invent your own hairstyles.

Pull up a chair

Clay people and animals sometimes need to sit down or take a nap. Remember, if you are adding people or animals to your furniture, the furniture legs must be strong enough to support them.

STOOL

To make this simple stool, attach three sausages to a pancake. Turn the stool over and press gently until it's steady.

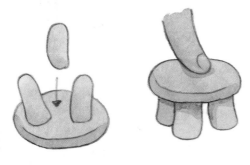

TABLES

Attach longer legs to a pancake and your stool becomes a table. Try using four legs or a drop-shaped base.

STRAIGHT-BACK CHAIR

Flatten an egg shape into a pancake and bend it. Add legs to the bottom as you did for the stool.

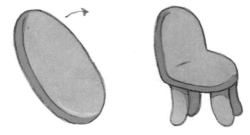

KITCHEN CHAIR

Attach a curved snake to the stool for a back. Add another snake in the center of the opening. Make sure the seat and legs are heavier than the back or your chair may topple.

ARMCHAIR

For a cozy armchair, start with a flat box shape. Add another box the same size. Stand up a thick pancake to make the back. Two thick cylinders form the arms and join the back and seat.

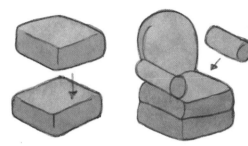

SOFA

Make a chair twice as wide for a sofa. Add some cushions and buttons if you like.

BED

Make a box shape. Add some pillows and two or four posts made of sausages with balls on top.

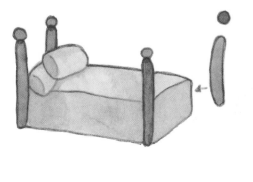

LAMPS

Press a ball of clay over your finger to make a lampshade. Pinch and turn it to make it even all around. Place the bowl over a lamp base. Experiment with different styles of bases and shades.

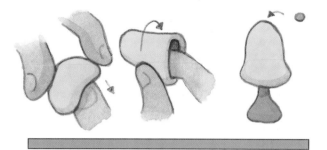

OTHER IDEAS

● Make some things to put on your tables. A thin snake around the edge of a pancake turns it into a plate.

● Press a ball of clay over your finger and pinch and turn it to make a bowl or a glass. Add a curved sausage handle for a cup.

● Make fruit out of balls and sausage shapes. What other food can you create?

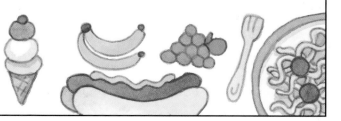

People movers

Hidden inside a blob of modeling clay is a whole fleet of fast-moving toys and vehicles.

SLED

Curl up the end of a fat ribbon to make a snow sled — or a magic carpet.

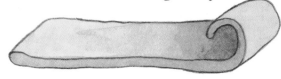

SKATEBOARD

Flatten a sausage. Pinch in the front end to a rounded point and add two cylinders for wheels. Turn up the back end and get ready to roll.

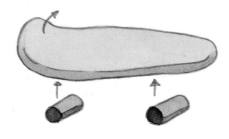

CAR

1 Start with a long box for the car body. Stick a smaller box on top.

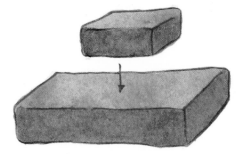

2 Attach four pancake wheels. The top half of each should attach to the car body and the bottom half should stick down below to hold the car up.

3 Make bumpers out of thin snakes. Add some pancake headlights and pancake hubcaps.

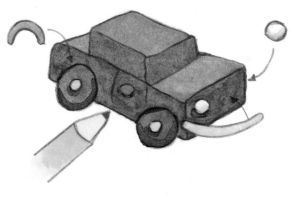

CUSTOM CARS

Experiment with body shapes to make your favorite cars. Change the wheel size, add some fancy stripes and details, or design a car of the past or future.

OTHER IDEAS

● Basic shapes can be combined to make trains, planes, buses and other people movers, too.

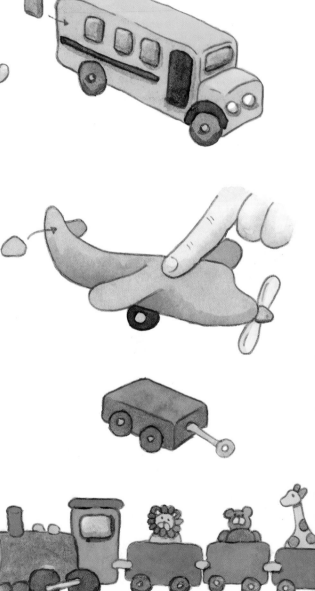

CONVERTIBLE

1 Start with a long box. Use a bent paper clip to scoop out the inside of the car, then add a pancake steering wheel.

2 Add a windshield and other details. Make some people from the waist up only and add them as passengers.

PICTURES

You can create any scene you can imagine with modeling clay. Plan your picture on paper first. Then build layer upon layer on a piece of stiff cardboard. Start with what is farthest away as your background.

The great outdoors

Begin an outdoor scene by deciding on a horizon line, where the sky and ground meet.

Choose a color for your sky. Spread a small lump of softened clay onto the cardboard. Add more pieces to cover the sky area with a thin, even layer. Extend the sky a little further down than you need.

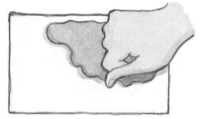

Mark a horizon line near the bottom edge of the sky. Along it press a ribbon of grass-colored clay. Smooth it down and fill in the rest of the ground with more clay.

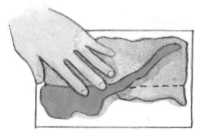

To make grass, gently scratch short lines on a green background with a fork or your fingernail.

Add a yellow or orange pancake sun, with triangles or thin snakes for rays. You can even stick on a face.

Overlapping a few pancakes of different sizes makes a fluffy cloud.

Press on small drop shapes to make rain. A zigzag ribbon becomes lightning.

For sand, dot a beige surface all over with a sharp pencil.

Want to make water? Scratch wavy lines on a blue background or press on some wiggly snakes for ripples.

Setting the scene

Once you've made an earth and sky background, you may want to add some other features. Here are some ideas to help you put plants and people into your picture.

1 Make individual blades of grass by cutting thin ribbons or snakes and pressing them down in layers.

2 For distant trees use pancakes with stems. Small bits of color make faraway flowers.

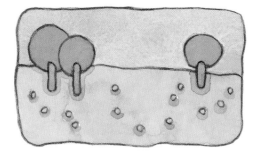

3 For a detailed tree, blend some sausage roots and snake branches onto a ribbon trunk. Texture the trunk with scratches or bumps. Cover your tree with leaves or fruit.

4 To make a fir tree, overlap triangle shapes from bottom to top on a small ribbon trunk. Small cuts on the edges will look like needles.

5 Most flowers need a snake stem and flat, pointy leaves. Make blossoms from rolled-up snakes or pancakes with tiny pancake centers.

6 For a more detailed flower, use small, flattened sausages for petals. If you want, draw veins on the leaves.

7 Add people to your scenes. To make sure they are the right size, sketch them into your background with a pencil first.

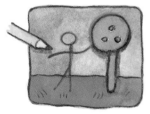 

8 People in pictures are almost the same as three-dimensional ones. (See page 20.) The difference is that the basic shapes are flat. Balls become pancakes, for example.

OTHER IDEAS

● Your pictures don't have to include earth and sky. Let your imagination take you many different places. Add some fish, rocks, seaweed, even mermaids to create an underwater scene.

● Try a picture that's out of this world! Create some planets, stars, astronauts and aliens.

Buildings

Clay boards and bricks can be pressed into place to build a doghouse, your house or even an outhouse!

1 Sketch a building outline into your clay background. Choose a color and press flat ribbons around the edges. Then fill in the inside.

2 Cut a ribbon into pieces and cover your building with these bricks. Or cover a house or castle in pancake-shaped stones.

3 Press on layers of overlapping ribbons to make a wooden house. Start at the bottom and work up. Some boards can join partway across. Add pencil dots for nails.

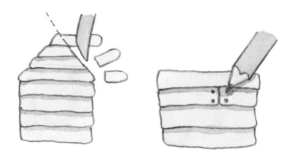

4 Add a shingled roof. Overlap rectangles of ribbon, starting at the lowest point of the roof and working up.

5 Make a thatched roof by scratching in a straw texture or adding layers of snakes.

6 Doors can be drawn on as outlines and filled in or shaped in your fingers and stuck on. To make a wooden door, line up strips of ribbon. Round balls make good doorknobs.

7 Experiment with window shapes and sizes. Thin snakes can be crisscrossed to make panes, flat ribbons can make window ledges or sills. Add a flower box if you like.

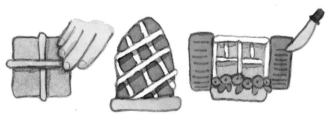

8 You can even make an igloo. Roll out a thin, flat piece of clay (make sure it doesn't stick to the table), cut out blocks of snow and fit them together.

9 Combine different shapes and textures to make all sorts of houses and buildings. Keep them plain or decorate them to create something fancy.

Home sweet home

You can set your picture indoors too. Here are some tips on creating the inside of a room.

Cover your picture surface with clay the color you want for your walls.

Create patterned wallpaper by adding snake stripes, polka dots or tiny flowers to the walls.

Alternate squares cut from two different colors of ribbon for a checkered floor. Or press some mixed-up marbled clay onto the floor.

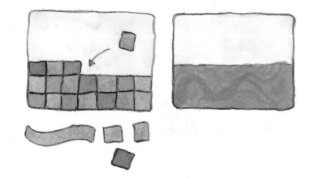

Decorate the walls of the room with pictures or press a pancake onto the wall and add dots and snakes to make a clock.

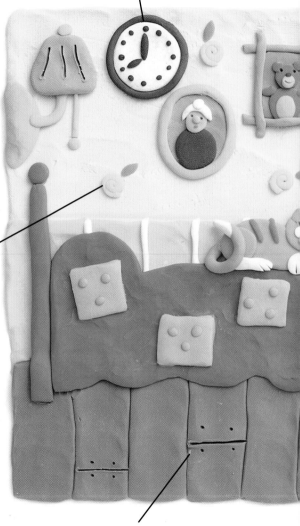

Make a wooden floor for a different look. Press flat ribbons down side by side. Dot on some nail holes.

Draw a window on the wall and scrape out the clay inside the shape. Fill the space with some sky and whatever else you might see out the window. Add curtains or a blind.

Use lots of different shapes to make furniture. See pages 26 and 27 for some ideas.

Coil up some multicolored snakes for a bedroom rug.

OTHER IDEAS

● Make a set and add three-dimensional characters to your flat picture background. Lay a shoe box flat and cut out and discard one long side. Cut a triangle from each end.

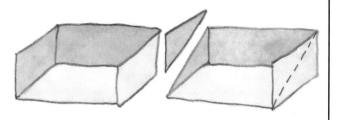

● Make a flat clay background on the bottom of the box. Stand the box up and cover the one long side in clay ground, grass or floor.

● Place your figures in the scene. You can even make other backdrops the same size and slide them into your box frame to change scenes.

3-D scenes

Clay coverings can transform empty containers and packages into model buildings and much more. Check to be sure that your clay will stick to the containers you've chosen.

1 Start with a cardboard base. A shallow box lid works well because it helps contain all the objects in your scene.

2 Find small cans and boxes, yogurt containers, bottle tops and other items that are the right shapes for what you want to make.

3 A milk carton is shaped like a house. Stuff it with scrunched-up newspaper for strength. Then cut off the top ridge and tape the carton shut.

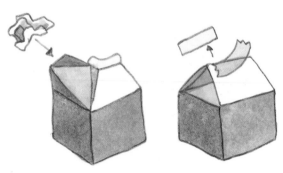

4 Firmly tape all the objects in your scene in position on the board. Do all the taping before adding any clay. (The oil in the clay will prevent the tape from sticking.)

5 When all the taping is done, carefully spread a base layer of very soft clay over each object.

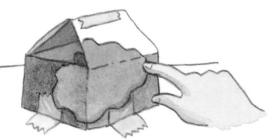

6 Once each object is covered, stick on boards, shingles, windows, a chimney and other details. See pages 34 and 35 for ideas.

7 Spread clay over the base of your landscape and add textures and shapes to finish off your scene.

OTHER IDEAS

Look for different shapes around your house to create rocket launchpads, farm scenes, cityscapes, prehistoric dinosaur hangouts … the possibilities are endless!

More ideas

Now that you've seen a little of what modeling clay can make, invent your own creatures and contraptions. Here are a few more ideas to get your imagination going.